MW01596882

TECH
bytes

HIGH-TECH

Solar Energy

by Meg Marquardt

NorwoodHouse Press

Cover: Solar panels harness solar energy and generate electricity.

Norwood House Press
Chicago, Illinois

For information regarding Norwood House Press, please visit our website at:
www.norwoodhousepress.com or call 866-565-2900.

PHOTO CREDITS: Cover: © Diyana Dimitrova/Shutterstock Images; © AJ_Watt/iStockphoto, 5; © Goddard Space Flight Center/NASA, 6; © Elena Elisseeva/Shutterstock Images, 28; © Ella Maru Studio/Science Source, 41; © Etienne Bouy/Sipa USA/AP Images, 32; © GraphicaArtis/Hulton Archive/Getty Images, 8; © James King-Holmes/Science Source, 23; © Katsumi Kasahara/AP Images, 19, 39; © Ke wei/Imagechina/AP Images, 35; © Lumppini/Shutterstock Images, 27; © Mark Agnor/Shutterstock Images, 43; © Novikov Aleksey/Shutterstock Images, 9; © palidachan/Shutterstock Images, 24; © Patrick Landmann/Science Source, 17; © Rudmer Zwerver/Shutterstock Images, 11; © seo byeong gon/Shutterstock Images, 37; © spainter_vfx/Shutterstock, 13; © Wilson Ring/AP Images, 31; © yangna/iStockphoto, 14

Content Consultant: Dr. Brandon Hathaway, Lead Research Scientist, Solar Energy Laboratory, University of Minnesota

Hardcover ISBN: 978-1-68450-916-4
Paperback ISBN: 978-1-68404-469-6

© 2020 by Norwood House Press.

Library of Congress Cataloging-in-Publication Data

Names: Marquardt, Meg, author.
Title: Solar energy / by Meg Marquardt.
Description: Chicago, Illinois : Norwood House Press, [2020] | Series: Tech
  Bytes: High-Tech | Audience: Grades 4 to 6. | Includes bibliographical
  references and index.
Identifiers: LCCN 2018054949 (print) | LCCN 2018055353 (ebook) | ISBN
  9781684044740 (ebook) | ISBN 9781684509164 (hardcover) | ISBN
  9781684044696 (paperback)
Subjects: LCSH: Solar energy--Juvenile literature.
Classification: LCC TJ810.3 (ebook) | LCC TJ810.3 .M325 2020 (print) | DDC
  621.47--dc23
LC record available at https://lccn.loc.gov/2018054949

319N–072019
Manufactured in the United States of America in North Mankato, Minnesota.

CONTENTS

Note: Words that are **bolded** in the text are defined in the glossary.

CHAPTER 1

Power from the Sun

A community is far away from a big city. That means it might not have access to clean water or health care. It also means residents probably don't have electricity. They live too far away from a central electrical **grid**.

However, this community might not need to be on the main grid. A company that makes solar panels is trying to light up the area. They bring in window-sized panels. They line them up outside where sunlight can hit the panels all day. The panels generate electricity and **charge** a battery. The battery is connected to wires strung through the community. Once the battery is charged, a resident tries to turn on a light. It works! Thanks to solar **power**, the community has electricity. Electricity can power water pumps in wells that help people get water. Farmers can use the electricity to pump water to crops.

Early Solar

Solar power comes from the Sun. The Sun is a large ball of gases kept hot by nuclear reactions. In the Sun, atoms combine to create new elements. The fusing of new elements, called nuclear fusion, gives off a lot of **energy** in all directions at all times. This energy takes the form of light. Some of it is visible light, while other kinds can't be seen by humans. When the light hits Earth's **atmosphere** and surface, some of it is absorbed as heat. This keeps Earth warm.

DID YOU KNOW?

In 2017, 1.3 percent of all energy in the United States came from solar power.

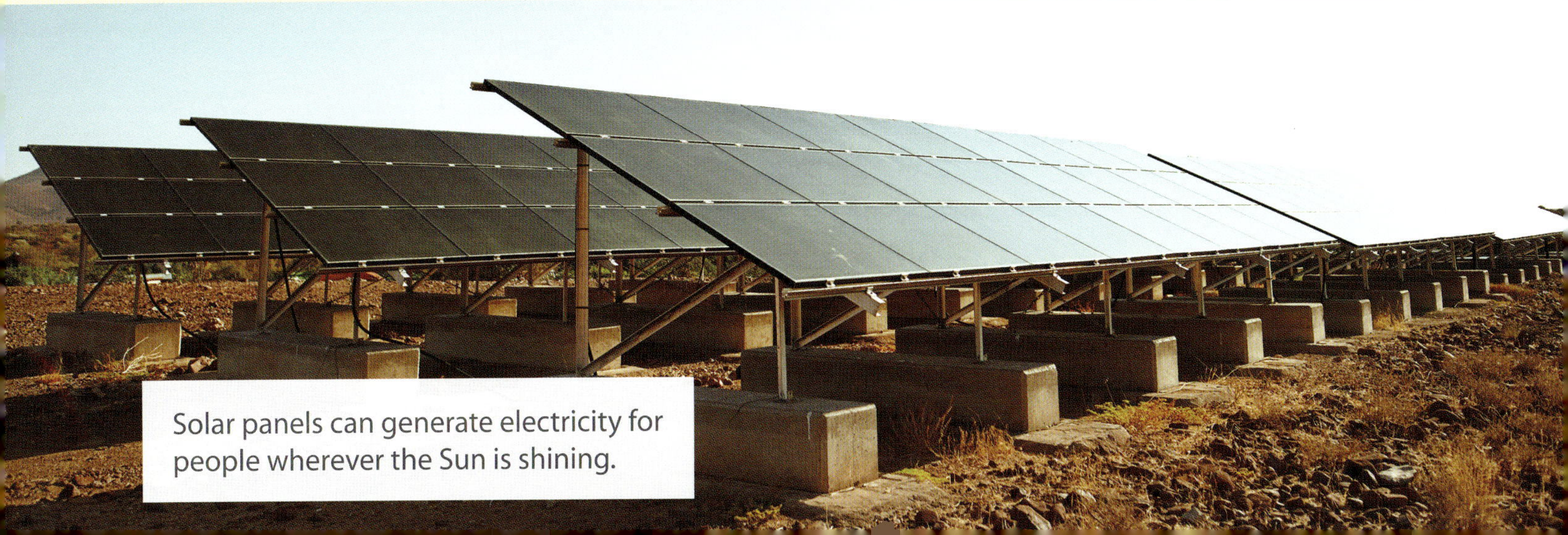

Solar panels can generate electricity for people wherever the Sun is shining.

During a solar flare, the Sun releases even more energy.

People have been trying to tap into the Sun's energy for a long time. Even in ancient times, Romans used sunlight to help heat bathhouses.

In the 1800s, scientists began trying to harness solar energy as a source of electricity. In 1839, French physicist Alexandre-Edmond Becquerel discovered the photovoltaic effect. He did so when he was only 19 years old. The photovoltaic effect occurs when light strikes certain materials and generates electricity. Becquerel used silver chloride. Other scientists tried using selenium. Silver chloride and selenium are both light sensitive and generate an electric current when exposed to light. Later, scientists put light-sensitive materials together to create what is known as a photovoltaic cell.

After Becquerel's discovery, many other scientists tried to create photovoltaic cells. Multiple cells could be joined together into a large, flat pane called a solar panel. One successful solar inventor was Charles Fritts. In 1884, Fritts created a group of solar panels that could be attached to a roof. With that invention, the modern solar power movement began.

Converting Energy

Early versions of solar panels didn't produce a lot of energy for their size. In fact, they produced so little that a typical solar panel couldn't power a

Ancient Uses of Solar Power

Solar power has been harnessed for thousands of years. Early civilizations built homes specifically to catch sunlight to help heat their homes. Ancient Romans built their famous bathhouses specifically with the Sun in mind. A bathhouse was built to catch afternoon sunlight, helping warm the waters for visitors. Large windows that let in a lot of sunlight have been used in architecture to help warm buildings for centuries.

Early solar panels were not very efficient. They could be combined to power small appliances.

simple household appliance. Even though sunlight was everywhere, the technology was not good enough to harness much of its energy.

In 1954, that changed. Two scientists at Bell Laboratory cracked the photovoltaic code. They created solar cells out of silicon. Silicon is a metalloid element. It has properties of both metals and nonmetals. It can be processed and cut into thin sections to make solar cells. The scientists at Bell Laboratory created a solar cell that was 4 percent efficient. That means it could convert 4 percent of the energy in sunlight into electricity. It might not seem like a lot. But it was much better than earlier cells. It was enough to power small devices. Soon after, the scientists created one that was 11 percent efficient.

Solar energy does not only come from photovoltaic cells that use visible light. Researchers have designed ways to

Concentrated solar power uses mirrors to gather light. This is another way to use solar power to generate electricity.

capture heat from both visible and invisible portions of sunlight, too. Capturing heat this way is solar thermal power. There are two ways technology harvests solar thermal power. Solar thermal collectors can come in panels, which look similar to photovoltaic panels, but absorb sunlight to heat water or air. The other type of solar thermal technology is called concentrated solar power. Concentrated solar power uses mirrors to reflect sunlight from a very large area and concentrate it onto a much smaller area. This helps part of the mirror reach higher temperatures than panels. These temperatures are high enough to boil water and make steam. The steam turns a **turbine** to make electricity.

The future seemed promising except for one big problem. Solar panels were very expensive to make for the amount of electricity they produced. Other sources of energy were much cheaper. For example, it is inexpensive for a coal plant to make a great deal of electricity. In order to be competitive, solar panels would have to be cheaper or more efficient.

Researchers began to look for cheaper ways to make solar cells. They shaped and cut panels in new ways that wasted less material. In the 1970s, the cost of solar panels had been cut in half. However, they still weren't very efficient.

Solar panels are around 30 percent efficient today and pack a big punch. They power houses and help power larger buildings. However, researchers are still working to make them even more cost effective and efficient. The future of solar energy depends on harnessing the energy solar panels already create.

The Future of Solar

Solar power is a **renewable** energy source. As long as the Sun is shining, solar panels can harvest its light for power. Renewable energy is important for the planet's future. Today's most common power sources are fossil fuels. These are nonrenewable energy sources. Once a fossil fuel, such as coal or oil, runs out, it is gone for good.

Fossil fuels get their name from actual fossils. When animals and plants die, their remains often end up underground. Over hundreds of millions of years, the bodies of prehistoric plants and animals were buried under more and more layers of land. The pressure from that land crushed and heated the remains, eventually turning them into oil, natural gas, and coal. Eventually, people realized that burning these materials produced energy.

Fossil fuels such as coal still generate more energy worldwide than solar energy.

Fossil fuels are burned to release the energy they contain. But this burning also releases greenhouse gases, such as carbon dioxide. Greenhouse gases trap heat in Earth's atmosphere. That heat has led to higher temperatures. This process, known as global warming, creates climate

DID YOU KNOW?

In 2018, some of the best solar panels converted about 45 percent of available solar energy.

Solar Power in Space

Even though solar panels were too expensive for everyday use in the 1950s, the United States government saw potential in the technology. One application was on satellites that were sent into space. In 1958, a Navy satellite called *Vanguard I* had solar cells. They were small, but they were able to power the satellite's radios. Within a decade, many spacecraft had some sort of solar panel technology. In 1964, a National Aeronautics and Space Administration (NASA) satellite called *Nimbus* was powered entirely with solar energy. Using solar power in space makes a lot of sense. It's hard or impossible to refuel satellites or replace their batteries. But solar power is free and unlimited. As long as the Sun shines on them, solar-powered satellites can keep working.

change. As Earth warms, problems like drought and severe weather will get worse.

Renewable energy, including solar power, might be the answer. After the panels have been made, solar energy production doesn't produce greenhouse gases. And the greenhouse-gas emissions from manufacturing panels are low.

Solar energy also won't run out. Of all the renewable energy sources, solar is the most abundant. All of the sunlight that hits Earth during one hour has enough energy to meet the energy needs of the entire world for a year. The future of solar power is figuring out how to capture more than just 20 to 30 percent of that power and finding better ways to store it for

There will always be an abundance of solar energy.

when it is needed. However, there are still challenges ahead. Scientists are trying to design cheaper, better, longer-lasting solar panels. Researchers are hard at work making widespread solar power a reality.

The Sun gives off energy in every direction in the form of light.

CHAPTER 2

Making Solar Panels Better

Energy comes in many forms, including electricity, heat, and light. An important aspect of energy is that one type can be turned into another. If researchers can create a device from the right materials, then light energy can be turned into electricity. That's just what solar panels are trying to do.

DID YOU KNOW?

Germany is the leader in solar power production. As of 2016, it produced twice as much as the United States.

How a Solar Panel Works

Solar panels create energy by generating an electric current. An electric current happens when small **particles** called electrons move. Electrons are one of the key types of particles in solar energy, along with photons.

Light is made up of photons. Photons can be absorbed by a surface. We are able to see because these particles are absorbed by our eyes. Photons can also bounce off a surface. Scientists are able to turn light into energy because of how these particles interact with surfaces.

A solar panel is made of layers that use these two types of particles. Electrons are found in atoms and have a negative charge. A solar panel's top layer is covered with a material that has a lot of electrons and a negative charge. The bottom layer is covered with a material that has fewer electrons and a positive charge. When sunlight shines on the solar panel, the photons in the light knock some of the electrons free. Those electrons rush through a wire to the positive-charged panel. The movement of these electrons is electricity. The electrons then return to the top layer of the panel, and the process repeats.

Creating Ideal Materials

The process of making energy from light seems simple. All it takes is getting electrons to move from one place to another. In reality, solar panel designers face a lot of challenges.

One challenge is finding the ideal material. Solar panels have to strike a balance. They have to be good at converting sunlight to electricity. But they also can't be too expensive. Finding a balance is difficult.

Most solar panels are made from a type of silicon. One way to make panels is to create long cylinders of silicon. Workers can then slice off thin layers of silicon called wafers. The wafers are laid together into cells and then into a panel. These panels can convert up to 23 percent of sunlight into electricity. However, a lot of expensive materials are lost when workers cut away unused sections from the wafers.

Another way to make panels is to shape melted silicon in a **mold**. The molded silicon is then cut into wafers. Less material is lost when working from

This is a silicon wafer. The process of making silicon wafers into solar cells is expensive.

these molds. However, the resulting solar cells are less efficient. They only convert around 20 percent of sunlight to electricity.

Researchers are hard at work trying to find inexpensive but effective materials. One avenue being explored is thin-film technology. This technique uses significantly thinner conductors, such as silicon, placed on glass or metal. These films can convert anywhere from 10 percent to almost 30 percent of sunlight into energy, depending on what conductor is used. And because the base material is glass or metal, they are much lighter and potentially cheaper to produce than both other forms of panels. However, many thin-film technologies require rare elements which may become more expensive as the technology becomes more popular.

Challenge of Storage

The Sun doesn't always reach solar panels. That's a problem for solar cell technology. At night, solar panels can't generate electricity. When it's cloudy, panels don't work as well. During the daytime, panels generate lots of electricity. But at this time, many people are at school or work. That means they aren't using electricity in their homes. Demand for electricity is low. Demand is highest in the evening, when people are at home. They are using it to cook dinner,

Thin-film panels are a new and promising avenue of solar power technology.

watch TV, and run lights. People tend to use most of their electricity when the Sun is setting.

To overcome this challenge, the electricity generated by panels needs to be stored. Batteries are one solution. Batteries convert electrical energy into chemical energy. When electric current goes into a battery, it charges the chemicals inside the battery. When electricity is needed later, the battery converts the energy from the chemicals back into electricity.

Batteries pose a few problems, though. One problem is that every time energy is converted from one form to another, some of the energy is lost. Since solar panels already only capture about 20 percent of sunlight, losing even more energy when using a battery is a problem. Also, batteries hold less and less charge over time. Because of these issues, improving battery life and efficiency is the focus of modern battery research.

Another way to store solar energy is a system called pumped storage. When the solar panels are generating more

Batteries are one option for storing solar-generated energy, but they also have drawbacks.

electricity than is needed, the excess energy is used to pump water uphill into a storage reservoir. When there isn't enough energy, some of that water is released back down. The movement of water spins turbines. The turbines change the kinetic energy of the rushing water into electrical energy. Pumped storage loses very little energy, so it is very efficient. However, it requires large reservoirs of water. These reservoirs take up a lot of room, and the amount of water needed is not always available.

Batteries and pumped storage are the two most popular options for energy storage, but the field is still developing. Many other possibilities are being researched. As new options are tested and improved, they will help advance the use of solar energy around the world.

Problems of Nature

Sometimes, solar energy challenges aren't just about materials and storage.

DID YOU KNOW?

From 2010 to 2017, the price of solar panels dropped 70 percent. That means that by 2017, it only cost around $17,000 to install solar panels on a home.

Protecting nature and wildlife can be an obstacle, too. Heat and light generated by mirrors used for concentrated solar energy can be harmful or even deadly to birds and other wildlife. Though concentrated solar energy does lead to bird deaths, fossil fuel mining and consumption kill birds at a higher rate.

Solar panels also don't work as well on super-hot days. When temperatures rise above 90 degrees Fahrenheit (32 degrees C), panels don't produce

Solar's Carbon Footprint

It takes energy to make a solar panel. Materials have to be mined using drills and other machines. Then, the materials have to be turned into panels. This process takes place in factories where energy is used for heating, molding, and cutting. Then, the panels have to be **installed**. Workers must drive to the site and use machinery to set up the panels. All of this work uses energy, and much of that energy comes from fossil fuels. These fossil fuels release greenhouse gases, including carbon dioxide. So even though solar panels produce clean energy, it takes some dirty energy to make them. That dirty energy is called a carbon footprint. It takes approximately two years of producing clean energy to offset a solar panel's carbon footprint. Considering the life of a panel, this carbon footprint is very low.

For solar panels to be as efficient as possible, they need to be cleaned regularly.

Solar Heating

Solar energy is used for more than electricity. Solar collectors trap heat from visible and invisible photons of sunlight and use that energy to heat water. Insulated pipes help water retain the heat on its way to a storage tank. The hot water can then be used for bathing and other needs. Solar heat can also be used in other ways. In the winter, it can help heat buildings. This cuts down on the fuel or electricity needed to run a heater.

as much energy. Solar panels also don't work as well if they are dirty. Dust and dirt can land on panels, making them less efficient. Cleaning a few panels on a roof is easy. But regularly cleaning a huge field of panels that help power a city takes a lot more work.

Researchers are working to find ways that solar panels can clean themselves. Some of the methods include automated nozzles or using static electricity. Automated nozzles spray the panels with soap and water to clean dirt. Users can set the nozzles on a schedule. Researchers are also looking into using static electricity to remove dust. An electrical charge moves from one side to the other, pushing the dust with static electricity. This could help keep panels even cleaner than washing them.

CHAPTER 3

Solar-Powered Cars, Houses, and Cities

Most people get their energy from the power grid. The power grid refers to all of the power lines that run throughout a city or rural area. These lines connect power plants to individual homes and businesses. Power companies produce the energy that people use. But solar power is changing how the grid works.

Solar-Powered Houses

One of the most common ways people use solar energy is to help power their homes with rooftop solar panels. The electricity generated may be stored in batteries or used right away. This power can heat water and run an air conditioner. It can power appliances such as refrigerators.

Most homes that have solar panels are still hooked into the power grid. Sometimes not enough solar power is stored during the day. When a family is home at night and needs a lot of energy, they might have to use energy from the grid. However, this energy exchange goes both ways. If the solar panels produce more electricity than the house needs, they may feed that power back into the grid. The power can then be used by other customers on the grid. In some places, the power company pays people for supplying this energy. This process is called net metering.

Solar panels don't work for all homes. Sometimes, trees or taller houses block the Sun. The best place to put solar panels

Power lines connect most homes and buildings to the power grid.

DID YOU KNOW?

One of the most common applications of solar panels is in calculators. Their tiny solar cells generate approximately 1.5 to 2.0 volts.

Solar panels are not a viable option for everyone due to housing situations.

Other Renewables

Solar power isn't the only renewable energy. Another type is wind energy. Large windmills are turbines built in windy places, often on plains or along the coast. As the turbines turn, they create electricity. Water moves other turbines in a similar way. As water from a river flows over the turbines, the motion generates electricity. Underground heat is another renewable energy source. The inside of the Earth is so hot that it creates steam as the heat moves to the surface. People capture that steam to create electricity or to heat a space. Renewable energy also comes from biomass, or natural waste. Examples are yard waste or materials left over from harvesting crops. When that waste is burned, it can be used to make steam to create electricity.

is typically on the south or west side of a house. Not all houses have a roof that faces south. Cost can also be a problem. Installing solar panels can cost as much as purchasing a car. In the United States, not all states offer benefits to a homeowner for using solar energy. Without net metering, it could be hard for some homeowners to afford solar panels. Luckily, more and more states are considering net metering as a way to promote solar energy. There are also programs that lease solar panels. The cost of the panels and installation is distributed over the lease.

Solar-Powered Cities

All kinds of buildings are getting a solar-powered boost. Some companies are using solar power in their offices. For example, when financial company TD Ameritrade built its new headquarters in 2013, it included solar power. The company's building houses 1,300 employees. It catches rainwater to use for things, like washing hands. Solar thermal collectors allow heat from the Sun's rays to warm that water directly.

Beyond single buildings, some cities are trying to incorporate more solar energy into everyday power use. Big cities that require lots of power might be a long way off from converting entirely to renewable energy sources. But some small towns have already made the leap to entirely green energy production.

For example, Burlington, Vermont, uses a mix of hydropower, wind, and solar to power the city. In 2016, the top city in the United States for solar panel installation was San Diego, California. It installed solar panels in business and school parking lots. San Diego produced enough energy to power 76,000 homes. San Diego has pledged to use only energy from renewable sources by 2035. That means installing even more solar panels and looking into other forms of renewable energy generation and storage. For large-scale projects, solar is almost always just one piece of the renewable energy puzzle.

Burlington, Vermont, purchased and operates a hydropower plant as part of its renewable energy goals.

Solar-Powered Vehicles

Solar power can also change the way people travel. Since 1987, a solar car competition has taken place in Australia every two years. In this competition, college students from around the world create a car that runs only on solar power. These cars travel across the Australian outback.

Some of this technology has hit the streets. A startup company in Munich, Germany, created a solar-powered car that can travel in a city. This car has solar panels on its hood, roof, and sides. It can be charged like a traditional electric car. It can also charge with the panels. After charging the battery, the car can continue to charge as the driver travels

Solar Impulse 2 demonstrated that solar power can be used for more than powering cars.

around town. The solar panels will continue to charge the battery as it is depleted from use, greatly extending the range of the electric car.

Cars aren't the only vehicles getting a solar makeover. In 2016, *Solar Impulse 2*, a solar-powered plane, made a trip around the world. It was a small, lightweight plane. It carried the pilot and only flew approximately 30 miles per hour (48 km/h). Through several flights, it spent more than 23 days in the air on solar power. The longest leg of the flight was a little under five days. The technology might not be ready for big passenger planes yet, but it is a good first step.

Trains are another form of transport getting a solar boost. In India, a passenger train uses solar power to light the cars and to power fans. The train still uses diesel gas to move, but using solar power for the cabins helps save more than 5,500 gallons (20,800 L) of diesel fuel per year.

? DID YOU KNOW?

In October 2018, the *Parker* solar probe reached a top speed of 153,545 miles per hour (247,107 km per hour). This is the fastest any man-made object has ever moved.

Solar Power on the Go

Solar power isn't only produced in big panels attached to houses or planes. Portable solar panels also exist. Some of these are for personal everyday use. Others help those who have lost power in the aftermath of natural disasters. These technologies can help solar go anywhere.

Many different outdoor activities can use solar-powered technologies. Solar-powered ovens use mirrors to heat up food. Flexible solar panels can be attached to the outside of a backpack. These panels can then be used to charge phones. Portable panels can charge cameras for nature photography, helping people take even more great pictures. For hikers, there are even solar-powered tents. These tents have solar panels in the tent material. This is great for camping during darker winter months. The solar power can help provide light after dark.

Large solar panels that can be rolled up are another innovation in portable solar technology. These flexible panels aren't

Recovery efforts after natural disasters require a lot of energy. Solar panels can help supply that energy, especially when the power grid is damaged.

Solar Power on Mars

Solar power is taking research to other planets. Some of the rovers on Mars utilize solar panels. Rovers are small robots that scientists use to study the planet's surface and atmosphere. NASA's rovers on Mars are named *Spirit* and *Opportunity*. They have wide arms that are covered with solar panels. The panels gather enough sunlight to let the rovers move around the planet's surface and conduct experiments. The solar panels charge a battery to store extra energy. Since the rovers are powered only by solar power, scientists have to be careful. They cannot drive the rovers into places without sunlight. Mars has lots of shady canyons. Because of this, Mars rovers focus on wide open spaces. The missions were planned for ninety days, but the rovers kept operating for years beyond expectations.

as efficient as stationary panels. However, because these panels can be rolled and unrolled multiple times, they have many different applications. For example, a natural disaster like a hurricane could knock out a power grid. Recovery workers could use more portable, flexible panels to replace power from the grid. These panels could also be used to help power recovery work far away from a traditional power source. A researcher conducting experiments in a remote desert area, for instance, could use these panels to help power scientific equipment.

CHAPTER 4

The Solar Power of the Future

From the early 1900s, solar power has come a long way. Panels are on top of houses. Cities have set up fields of panels in parking lots and open spaces to catch some rays. Mirrors concentrate light onto towers in deserts. As solar technologies become better at catching the Sun, they may help pave the way for a fossil-fuel free future.

Cities are finding innovative places to increase their solar energy production, even using parking lots.

Game-Changing Materials

On the horizon are new materials that might help solar power break into the mainstream. Researchers are trying to create more efficient and cheaper materials. Such materials could help generate more electricity and make solar a more desirable option for homeowners and energy companies. **Organic** solar cells might be the answer to both challenges.

Organic solar cells are made of polymers. Polymers are molecules strung together to make plastics or rubbers. These polymers can absorb light or are covered with materials that absorb light. Absorbing light kickstarts the process of moving electrons.

Materials for silicon cells have to be mined. But polymers can be made in a lab. That means organic solar cells are cheaper and easier to produce. Also, since they are made of plastics, some organic solar cells are flexible. Instead of having to be set on a flat surface, these cells could

DID YOU KNOW?

In the United States, solar panels prevent 81.5 million tons (73.9 mT) of carbon dioxide emissions a year. That's equal to planting 1.9 billion trees.

go anywhere. They could wrap around light poles, for example.

Unfortunately, organic solar cells are less efficient than silicon solar cells. For the most part, organic solar cells are about 10 percent efficient. That's only half as efficient as silicon cells. However, in 2018, one organic solar cell reached 15 percent efficiency. Though that's still

DID YOU KNOW?

In 2018, there were enough solar panels in the United States to power 11 million homes.

Organic solar cells can be flexible.

less than a silicon solar cell, it's a big leap forward.

Perovskite cells are another promising technology. Perovskite refers to a specific structure of a material. Lots of different minerals and materials can be made into a perovskite, as long as the molecules form a particular cube-like structure.

In 2009, researchers reported that perovskites might make good solar panels. At that time, perovskite panels were only 3.8 percent efficient. But in 2018, that efficiency had jumped to

Unusual Solar Technologies

Solar panels have found their ways to strange places. Some windows have been turned into solar panels. These windows let some of the light through while capturing the rest. Such windows could be used in offices and schools to add a boost of energy. Solar panels have also been used to power vaccine refrigerators. Vaccines are medicines that help protect against certain illnesses. However, vaccines have to be kept at a cool temperature. This has been a problem when trying to transport vaccines in hot climates to small towns and villages. But mobile solar panels can power small refrigerators, making sure vaccines stay cool during transport.

The structure of perovskites makes for good solar cells.

Solar Power on the Moon

Cloudy days can prevent solar panels from charging. The Moon, though, doesn't have cloudy days. It might sound farfetched, but scientists are thinking about putting solar panels on the Moon. When the Moon's solar panels collect electricity, they could convert that energy to a form called microwaves. This is the same energy used to cook food in a microwave. Antennas could beam the microwaves to collectors on Earth. The solar panels could be constructed and maintained by robots that stay on the Moon. The biggest hurdle is the cost of such a program. It might be so expensive that no single country could pay for it. It would have to be an international effort.

over 20 percent. With such fast gains in solar efficiency, a maximum possible efficiency of approximately 31 percent, and a much lower production cost than other solar panel types, perovskites might be the future of solar energy. They can potentially work on any surface facing the Sun. However, researchers aren't yet sure how to make perovskite solar cells on a large scale.

Solar Power's Place in Energy Production

One thing that remains unclear is just how popular solar energy will be in the future.

In 2017, researchers thought that solar power would increase to 16 times its 2017 production by 2040. With concerns about climate change growing, people will look for more ways to offset their carbon footprints. Advances in technology and demands for clean energy might mean solar power becomes a mainstream power source for the world even faster.

One thing is for sure: Solar power is here to stay. With the need for renewables growing every year, researchers will keep searching for the best materials to make efficient cells. It might not be too long before solar panels help power everything from cell phones to cars.

With all the research going into solar panels, solar energy will definitely be part of the future of energy production.

DID YOU KNOW?

The desire for solar energy is a widespread phenomenon. Every 100 seconds, a new solar installation goes in somewhere in the United States.

atmosphere (AT-muhss-fihr): The gases that surround a planet.

charge (CHARJ): To store up energy for later use.

energy (EN-ur-jee): The potential to perform work or create heat, which comes in forms such as electrical, chemical, and thermal.

grid (GRID): The wires and cables that energy flows through from power plants to homes and businesses.

installed (in-STAWLD): To put something into place, such as attaching solar panels to a roof.

mold (MOHLD): An empty container that liquid can be poured into to make a specific shape.

organic (or-GAN-ik): Material made from living matter.

particles (PAR-tuh-kuhls): Small pieces of matter or energy.

power (POU-ur): A rate of production, consumption, or movement of energy.

renewable (ri-NOO-uh-bul): Energy that comes from a source that doesn't need to be replenished, such as energy from the Sun.

turbine (TUR-bine): A machine connected to a generator that helps turn motion into electricity.

FOR MORE INFORMATION

Books

Diane Bailey. *Solar Power*. Mankato, MN: Creative Education, 2015. Learn about ways that solar power has been harnessed in the past, notable discoveries, and the obstacles solar energy faces.

Laurie Brearley. *Solar Power: Capturing the Sun's Energy*. New York: Children's Press, 2019. Read about how sunlight travels 93 million miles to Earth and about the technology that harnesses its power.

Steven Otfinoski. *Wind, Solar, and Geothermal Power: From Concept to Consumer*. New York: Children's Press, 2016. Read this book to learn about how scientists and engineers are working to create new energy options.

Websites

EIA Energy Kids: Renewable Solar (https://www.eia.gov/kids/energy.php?page=solar_home-basics) This government website teaches kids about solar energy and different ways to convert it to electricity.

Let's Go Solar: Solar Power for Kids (https://www.letsgosolar.com/consumer-education/solar-project-for-kids/) This page has solar-powered projects to teach kids about solar power.

NASA Climate Kids: Renewable Energy (https://climatekids.nasa.gov/menu/renewable-energy/) This website from NASA teaches kids about the solar power industry and global warming.

INDEX

Meg Marquardt started her career as a scientist but decided she liked writing about science even more. She enjoys researching physics, geology, and climate science. She lives in Madison, Wisconsin, with her two scientist cats, Lagrange and Doppler.